The Fools' Manual

The Fools' Manual

A Study and Practice Guide
for *Foolish Church: Messy, Raw, Real, and Making Room*

Lee Roorda Schott

CASCADE *Books* • Eugene, Oregon

THE FOOLS' MANUAL
A Study and Practice Guide for *Foolish Church: Messy, Raw, Real, and Making Room*

Copyright © 2019 Lee Roorda Schott. All rights reserved. Except for brief quotations in critical publications or reviews, and reproduced "Practicing Foolishness" pages as authorized herein, no part of this book may be reproduced in any manner without prior written permission from the publisher. Write: Permissions, Wipf and Stock Publishers, 199 W. 8th Ave., Suite 3, Eugene, OR 97401.

Cascade Books
An Imprint of Wipf and Stock Publishers
199 W. 8th Ave., Suite 3
Eugene, OR 97401

www.wipfandstock.com

PAPERBACK ISBN: 978-1-5326-9045-7
HARDCOVER ISBN: 978-1-5326-9046-4
EBOOK ISBN: 978-1-5326-9047-1

Cataloguing-in-Publication data:

Names: Schott, Lee Roorda, 1963, author.

Title: The fools' manual : a study and practice guide for *Foolish Church: Messy, Raw, Real, and Making Room* / Lee Roorda Schott.

Description: Eugene, OR: Cascade Books, 2019.

Identifiers: ISBN 978-1-5326-9045-7 (paperback) | ISBN 978-1-5326-9046-4 (hardcover) | ISBN 978-1-5326-9047-1 (ebook)

Subjects: LCSH: Church work. | Religious life—Christianity. | Study guide.

Classification: BV4465 .S68 2019 (paperback) | BV4465 (ebook)

Manufactured in the U.S.A.   09/11/19

All scripture quotations are from the New Revised Standard Version Bible, copyright © 1989 National Council of the Churches of Christ in the United States of America, nrsvbibles.org. Used by permission. All rights reserved worldwide.

Quotations are reprinted from *Foolish Church: Messy, Raw, Real, and Making Room*, © 2019 Lee Roorda Schott. All rights reserved. Used by permission.

Contents

Introduction | vii

SESSION 1
The Church Doesn't Need Us to Hide Our Scars | 1

SESSION 2
The Church Is More about Relationships Than Programs | 11

SESSION 3
The Church Believes and Protects | 21

SESSION 4
The Church Builds Boundaries, Not Walls | 31

SESSION 5
The Church Brings Its Messes into the Light | 42

SESSION 6
The Church Has Something Critically Important to Offer | 52

About the Author | 61

Introduction

A *Fools'* Manual, really? Has no one ever dared call you a "fool" before? Well then, I'm happy to be the first!
(Then again, I'm probably not.) (The first, I mean.)
(And, after all, *you're* the one who picked up the book!)
Here's the thing: *I mean it as a compliment.* Like I said in *Foolish Church*, we must be some kind of fools to be able to glimpse the wisdom of God. Congratulations for joining that quest. We're the ones who get it: None of this is foolishness *at all*. It's deadly serious, and important, and worthy. Thank you for joining me in believing that.

Usually a book like this one would be called something like a Study Guide. Someone writes a six-chapter book and soon they'll issue a Study Guide, or even just a Leader's Guide, intended to help a small group of readers utilize the book in a Sunday school class or other gathering across six hour-long sessions. Why not call it that?

Here's why. I didn't write *Foolish Church* just for you to *read* it. I wrote *Foolish Church* for people foolish enough to actually *do* it. You fools don't need a study guide; you need a crash helmet!

And perhaps a manual to help you wrestle with *how*.

Foolish Church, and this manual, are written for people like you and churches like yours, who are realizing the way we've been doing church isn't enough. You are holding this book because you wonder how we can focus less on sparkle and more on grit. You've sensed that the way we've packaged and sold our churches—and the gospel—has left a lot of people behind, disconnected, and marginalized. You see a certain wisdom in words like *raw*, *real*, and *messy* (even though they may scare you) and you're foolish enough to imagine giving them a try.

Introduction

You could share this vision by working through this manual with a Sunday school class or any church-based small group. If you have a courageous leadership team or missions committee, bring it to them. The manual will even guide you as an individual, if you're not ready to invite a larger conversation, but I'll warn you: the practice instructions will expect you to interface with other human beings.

"Practice instructions," you say? Yes, that's part of this manual! Each session includes a set of "Practicing Foolishness" prompts that I hope will lead you into *doing* what you read about in *Foolish Church*. Some are thought experiments. Some are conversation starters that range from easy to edgy, including some that will push you right out of your comfort zone. There are directions for role-playing to help you work through the kinks and the awkwardness of how to say things. You'll find suggestions for bringing these ideas to your pastor or other church leaders. You won't be able to complete most of these activities in any specific class time; they'll keep you busy between sessions and, I hope, for a long time after you've worked through this manual.

"Interface with other human beings," you say? As I was writing the foolishness prompts, I found myself worrying for you introverts who will read this manual. An introvert myself, I realize some of us will cringe at the many conversations and group activities I suggest. I don't see an alternative, though, if we want to accept the gospel imperative of loving our neighbor. It will push us. We'll have to be foolish enough to let it.

Pondering this, it has occurred to me that Jesus may well have been an introvert. Think about it. Sure, he traveled with crowds and spoke to thousands, across years of ministry. But when he needed to recharge, he went apart, by himself, for silence and prayer. He surrounded himself with a small number of close friends, of which an even smaller number—Peter, James, and John—appear to have formed an inner circle. There's a relational depth and intimacy in Jesus' story that looks familiar to this introvert.

Most of us, like Jesus, have learned to function well in a world where interaction in groups of people—even large ones—allows us to pursue the work to which we are called. We'll go apart to recharge; we get to claim that time. But when there's good reason for us to gird up our loins and face into the crowds, never believe it's too much for us! I'm asking you to be *that* foolish.

Introduction

Part of the foolishness is acknowledging—and I do—that we'll have to figure this out as we go along. My church inside prison has lived these ideas, and I've seen the need for them in my experience with churches outside the razor wire. But I haven't yet implemented most of them in an existing "outside" church. There we'll find people who come (like we do) carrying their own expectations and patterns built up over years and decades of church life that have been foolish in a different way. You and I will go on this adventure, and we'll learn a lot along the way. Let's be fools together.

Which reminds me: *you are invited to join a Foolish Church community* that I hope will support one another, share experiences and learnings, and celebrate successes as we pursue this foolishness. We'll connect using the hashtag **#FoolishChurch** on social media; I'm already thinking about how to award you for completing a certain number of foolishness prompts and posting or tweeting about your experiences. Stay tuned on my website (leeschott.com) and the Foolish Church page on Facebook for this news, and about in-person and virtual gatherings that will no doubt happen in time.

Let the foolishness persist.

A word to group leaders

This manual is arranged in six sessions. It can be used to guide a group through six gatherings of sixty or ninety minutes. Each session includes:

- opening questions and prayer (10–20 minutes),
- some reflection about the assigned chapter of *Foolish Church* (20–30 minutes),
- Bible exploration (15–20 minutes), and
- closing reflection, intentions, and prayer, including review of the "Practicing Foolishness" prompts mentioned above (15–20 minutes).

There's space for jotting responses and keeping track of foolishness prompts as you complete them. It will be helpful but perhaps not a necessity for each participant to have a copy of the manual in addition to a copy of *Foolish Church*. (If you are leading a group, you are welcome to reproduce the "Practicing Foolishness" prompts for that session for any member who does not have the manual.)

Foolish Church, and the questions in this manual, are aimed at how we do life together as communities of Christian faith, but this foolishness will

Introduction

also be of interest to persons disconnected from (or perhaps disillusioned with?) church. If you are part of a book club or other small group—or just want to pull some friends together—you can certainly adapt the learnings and practices for your purposes, and I'd love to hear from you about your experience doing so.

There's so much more I'd like to say to you if you are going to work through this manual in a series of group meetings. Here are a few points I'd urge you to keep in mind:

- It will be helpful if someone will take responsibility for preparing to lead each session. It could be a different person each time.
- Before your group meeting, take the time to familiarize yourself with the assigned chapter of *Foolish Church*, as well as the questions in this *Fools' Manual*.
- You'll have to make decisions about how to spend the time available; there's probably not time to cover every question. It will be helpful if you map out some estimated times for each part of the session, so you'll be ready to move the discussion along if needed. If time is short, consider devoting two gathering times to each session. Or you could invite participants to do some homework (such as the Bible questions) before they come.
- When you talk about a question (such as the beginning question for each session), you'll need to decide whether or not to have each participant answer, one at a time, with the whole group listening. In larger groups, it may work better (and save time) to have persons share their answers within a table group of four to six people or, if you aren't at tables, in groups of two or three who are sitting close together.
- If you have group members who don't know each other well, invite all—in the early sessions at least—to give their first name every time they speak during your class time. Soon all will know every other participant's name, which is a great win for community during and after your group.
- *Do* make room for each person to speak. Resist the temptation to move on, or to supply your own answer, if a question is met with silence. Trust that people are thinking, and leave room for those who need more time to process before they're ready to speak. Don't let your own anxiety about silence shut down what might become fruitful conversation.

Introduction

- Remind participants that the "practicing foolishness" prompts are the core of this manual. They're an integral part of each session, even though they'll (mostly) have to be completed outside of your group's gathering. Leave some time before each session ends for participants to commit to one or more prompts that they'll follow this week, and take a little time to hear some reports on those efforts when you gather again.

Finally, please encourage participants to connect with me on my website at leeschott.com, via Twitter @revleeesq, and at my Foolish Church page on Facebook. Snap a photo of your group—or of your foolish efforts—and send it to me, or post it on social media with information about your group and where you're from, with the hashtag **#FoolishChurch**! You (and they) are always welcome to email me at foolishchurch@gmail.com.

A note on pronouns

If you read all the way to the end of *Foolish Church*, you'll remember my comments about pronouns and my use of "she," "her," and "hers" for every ungendered character. That seemed right when I wrote those words two years ago. But in this *Fool's Manual*, I've adopted a different practice for two reasons: First, this manual speaks more about people out in the world than about the women I meet in prison, so it feels important to be more inclusive. And second, "they," "them," and "theirs" have become, since that writing, more accepted as inclusive pronouns for one or multiple persons, including those who identify as non-binary. Thus, those terms—"they," "them," and "theirs"—are my default in this volume, with the hope that we might find these words generous enough to include ourselves and all others.

(Of course, if you were to use female pronouns when you role-play some of the ungendered figures I describe, it sure would bring a smile to my face!)

Session 1
The Church Doesn't Need Us to Hide Our Scars

> Church is a gathering of real people who bring all that they are, their whole selves, with tears and laughter, scars and beauty, their uniqueness as well as their common humanity. When we look down those rows, we realize we're seeing beautiful, amazing children of God.
>
> *Lee Roorda Schott*

The Fools' Manual

Beginning

A question for entering this session:

> Tell briefly about a scar, blemish, or tattoo you have somewhere on your body, and the story behind it.

This session focuses on the Introduction and chapter 1 of *Foolish Church*. The Introduction introduces Lee Roorda Schott and Women at the Well, the church inside the Iowa women's prison that is the context for the learnings she shares. Chapter 1 invites us to notice that our churches often haven't been very welcoming to those who are scarred and hurting, which means many life experiences have been largely excluded or hidden in our midst.

A prayer as we open this time:

> O God, we are your beautiful people, and we have scars that bear witness to our rich, complicated, and sometimes painful lives. Help us bring that truth to this time today. Help us imagine loving one another foolishly enough that we would not turn away from each other's scars. Help us be a church that loves the way Jesus asks us to. Amen.

From the book

What stories or ideas in the Introduction and chapter 1 of *Foolish Church* particularly spoke to you? Challenged you? Inspired you?

Does your church have lines between life experiences that can and those that must not be shared? What are some of them? How do you know?

The Church Doesn't Need Us to Hide Our Scars

Read this excerpt from page 10 of *Foolish Church* and then consider the questions that follow:

> We could worry that we can't handle all those scars. The unveiling of their hurt might unearth ours. How much better to keep pain at a distance, where it seems like it can be controlled! So long as scars are only occasionally visible, we can think that they happen only to other people, and we might even convince ourselves that those people bear the blame for what happened. We would rather not face into the ways that life is unfair and justice incomplete. If we are brought face to face with the truth that scars are all around us—even *in* us—the world must be unsafe, and our mechanisms for comfort and security unveiled as illusions.

1. What feelings arise in you when you see a visible scar on another person, or when you hear about something tragic that happened to them?

2. Can you think of a time when hearing about someone else's hardship made *you* feel less safe? Explore those feelings.

3. Is life fair? If so, how do you account for the suffering that befalls people for no apparent reason? If not, how do you live with (or shield yourself from) that unfairness?

4. Is protecting ourselves from our own pain a good reason for our churches to put up barriers against people sharing their scars?

5. How would your church be different if, as Lee says at page 11, *"We get to bring our whole selves to church"*?

From the Bible

Read and consider the Bible excerpt and reflection in the box at page 14 of *Foolish Church*.

Read these words from John 20 (and perhaps John 20:19–31 for context) and consider the questions that follow:

> 26A week later his disciples were again in the house, and Thomas was with them. Although the doors were shut, Jesus came and stood among them and said, "Peace be with you." 27Then he said to Thomas, "Put your finger here and see my hands. Reach out your hand and put it in my side. Do not doubt but believe."

1. Does it surprise you to realize the risen Jesus has scars from the crucifixion?

2. Surely Jesus could have been raised with a new body, without blemish. Why might it be important that he maintains his scars, even in resurrection?

3. How can scars be a resource for ministry?

4. Consider one or more of these biblical figures and how their scars and challenging life experiences shaped them for the work God had for them. (In each case, the listed verses are a small part of a much larger biblical story. You may wish to read further for context and to consider additional experiences that shaped them.)

   Jacob. Genesis 32:22–32

   Moses. Exodus 2:11–15

   Job. Job 1.1–2.7

   Jeremiah. Jeremiah 38:1–16

   Mary Magdalene. Luke 8:2

   Peter. Luke 22:54–62

   Paul. Acts 7:54–8:3

   John of Patmos. Revelation 1:9

Closing

Review the "Practicing Foolishness" prompts below. If you're in a group, consider trying one of the role-playing scenarios in 1E before you close your time together. Commit to one or more of the foolishness prompts you personally will do to practice what we explored in this session.

If you're in a group, share prayer requests and be in prayer for one another during the coming week.

A prayer for ending each session:
> Holy and healing God, help us to trust you as we practice foolish love and ministry, this week and beyond. Send us out with courage and curiosity. Let us see those we meet with the eyes and grace of our Savior Jesus, in whose name we pray. Amen.

Practicing Foolishness

Here are some ideas for practicing the learnings of this section of *Foolish Church*. It will require some foolishness for us to actually *do* the things Lee describes. Let these prompts get you started and spark your own reckless imagination.

small folly

____**1A** Try this exercise with at least two small groups within your church, and see what conversation ensues. It's called "OK to say?" Pose this question: "For each of these sets of life experiences, if they happened to you, would it be OK to talk about them within your church, as a prayer request, or within a small group?" Pay attention to which scenarios make people less comfortable, and take time to wonder what it says about your church and your support for one another when the answer is "no." What would it take to move closer to "yes"?

- Your daughter has a baby. OK to say?
- Your daughter's baby is in the NICU. OK to say?
- Your daughter's baby has fetal alcohol syndrome. OK to say?

- You are having knee surgery. OK to say?
- You are going on dialysis. OK to say?
- You are having gastric bypass surgery. OK to say?

- You got diagnosed with lupus. OK to say?
- You just got diagnosed with cancer. OK to say?
- You just got diagnosed with HIV. OK to say?

- You just lost your job. OK to say?
- Your car just got repossessed. OK to say?
- You just became homeless. OK to say?

- You just got charged with speeding, twelve mph over the speed limit. OK to say?
- You just got arrested for driving while intoxicated. OK to say?
- Your license just got suspended for repeated moving violations. OK to say?

- Your sister is incarcerated in a different state. OK to say?
- Your dad is on the sex offender registry. OK to say?
- You have just been released on bond on an embezzlement charge. OK to say?

____**1B** When someone in real life tells you something painful or scary, pay attention how you are tempted to respond. Where do you feel anxiety in your body? Are you tempted to minimize their pain or to change the subject?

The Fools' Manual

____**1C** Spend some time with a person whom you know is dealing with a challenging circumstance. Pay attention to the conversation you have with them. Is it all about what they're going through? If so, why? Were you responding to their need or yours?

becoming reckless

____**1D** Spend some time with a person who you know is dealing with a challenging circumstance (as in 1C). In the spirit of Lee's words at page 13—"We don't let scars define one another"—do something, or ask something, that reminds you and that person they are more than this thing they're going through.

____**1E** Invite a friend or a small group to practice role-playing one or more of these scenarios. In each case, work on responding with unflinching attention and acceptance, without changing the subject and without trying to solve the person's problem or talk them out of how they feel. Practice asking open and non-leading questions, to help them come to speech about what's happening to them. Debrief with your friend or small group, and maybe practice a second time, perhaps changing roles this time, noticing how this feels and where it's hard.

- A good friend tells you, "I'm thinking about having some plastic surgery."
- Someone tells you, "I just got diagnosed with HIV."
- Someone you don't know at church leans over and says to you, "I just found out my dad is living out of his car; he's homeless."
- You notice the bruises on someone's face and, when you ask if she's OK, she begins to cry. She might go on to talk about an abusive partner, or her own failing eyesight, or her autistic teenager who is growing more physically unmanageable.

____**1F** When someone in real life tells you something painful or scary, practice responding with unflinching openness (as Lee describes at pages 12–13 of *Foolish Church*). How does it feel to stand by them as they face into this hard moment?

____**1G** Sit down with someone you know well and talk about *Foolish Church* and this session. Tell them you want to share something of your own story that you've kept hidden. If that person consents, and recognizing you don't control what happens next, dare to say out loud something about yourself that crosses the "respectability" lines we have discussed in this session. Notice how this feels and how the other person does or does not respond.

extreme foolishness

____**1H** Spend an hour or more in a place where you'll meet people you don't know, who might have something to say if you're open to it, and be present without spending time on your phone or in a book. Be curious but don't be intrusive, and see what conversations happen. Conduct yourself with unflinching openness and gentle curiosity. Some possibilities: Ride public transportation. Sit in a hospital waiting room, or at the Department of Motor Vehicles, or in a courthouse.

____**1I** Talk to your pastor about the possibility of sharing publicly about a scar you carry. Don't inflict your unresolved woundedness on the congregation (*Foolish Church*, page 11). But see how it might make a difference within your faith community if you took the lead in sharing out loud about something people don't know you have experienced.

____**1J** _____
_____
_____
_____

____**1K** _____
_____
_____
_____

(This is your space to devise your own prompts, and then to practice them. How foolish will you get?)

So, what did you do? What worked, and what felt like it didn't? What did you learn? How foolish were you?! Take time to share your experiences and your J and K prompts by reporting on Facebook or Twitter

The Fools' Manual

using this hashtag: **#FoolishChurch**. *Don't forget to check for others' ideas posted there as well. Lee will collect the best of these and share them on the Foolish Church page.*

It is an exquisite gift when another human being entrusts us with their truth. Let us hold it ever so gently.

Lee Roorda Schott

Session 2

The Church Is More about Relationships Than Programs

> Love has never become our normal response to other human beings.
>
> *Lee Roorda Schott*

The Fools' Manual

Beginning

A question for entering this session:

> Tell about a relationship you're glad (and perhaps surprised) to have been blessed by, that began in the context of church.

Share briefly about the foolishness prompts from session 1 that you (or others) tried. What happened? What did you learn?

This session centers on chapter 2 of *Foolish Church*, which wants us to focus on relationship—actually knowing and caring about one another—as the starting point for everything we do as a church. Relationship before programs. Relationship that helps each person know they matter.

A prayer as we open this time:

> O God, we are your beautiful people, and we find that our beauty emerges in relationship with one another. Help us bring that truth to this time today. Let us imagine loving one another foolishly enough to be in real, meaningful relationship with other human beings beyond our families and beyond our regular circle of friends. Help us be a church that loves the way Jesus asks us to. Amen.

From the book

What stories or ideas in chapter 2 particularly spoke to you? Challenged you? Inspired you?

The Church Is More about Relationships Than Programs

List some of the programs your church offers and mission and outreach projects that get promoted there.

Read this excerpt from page 21 of *Foolish Church* and then consider the questions that follow:

> Our missions take on an ominous *us* and *them* message. We get set up as generous helpers for *them* ("those people"), who desperately need us. We get to be the heroes. We have expertise, time, and money that we graciously bestow on recipients we hope will appreciate what we've done. We feel proud of what we've accomplished. But we don't learn very much when mission happens this way. It doesn't occur to us that "those people" might have wisdom and creativity that could enrich us, were we to know them. We rarely include them in the design and execution of our mission plan. Along the way, "those people" begin to internalize our message that they don't have anything to offer, which leaves them increasingly dependent and unlikely to volunteer the resources and wisdom they carry.

1. Describe a time when you were proud of yourself for the good deed you were doing for someone "less fortunate." (C'mon! You can admit it!)

2. Can you think of a time when your mission or program brought you into contact with a recipient and a meaningful, ongoing relationship began? What made it possible that time (or, if you can't think of one, why wasn't it possible)?

3. Would you rather (1) design a program to fix a person's problem, or (2) sit and learn from them about that problem? Why? Which feels harder?

4. Do you already have enough friendships? Does it feel like too much trouble to develop new relationships with persons whom you might know through church? Could you imagine Jesus calling you to love people you haven't met yet?

5. How would your church and its programs be different if, as Lee says at page 27, *"The first and best thing we do as a church is enter into real relationships with real human beings"*?

From the Bible

Read and consider the Bible excerpt and reflection in the box at page 31 of *Foolish Church*.

Read these words from Acts 6, which describe some challenges in the program of distributing food within the earliest Christian community, and then consider the questions that follow:

> 1Now during those days, when the disciples were increasing in number, the Hellenists complained against the Hebrews because their widows were being neglected in the daily distribution of

The Church Is More about Relationships Than Programs

food. 2And the twelve called together the whole community of the disciples and said, "It is not right that we should neglect the word of God in order to wait on tables. 3Therefore, friends, select from among yourselves seven men of good standing, full of the Spirit and of wisdom, whom we may appoint to this task, 4while we, for our part, will devote ourselves to prayer and to serving the word." 5What they said pleased the whole community, and they chose Stephen, a man full of faith and the Holy Spirit, together with Philip, Prochorus, Nicanor, Timon, Parmenas, and Nicolaus, a proselyte of Antioch. 6They had these men stand before the apostles, who prayed and laid their hands on them.

1. What is the program and what is the challenge the twelve are trying to solve?

2. Could the twelve have viewed this challenge as a question of relationships? How might that have led to a different response?

3. Is relationship central to the programs the church undertakes? Should it be?

4. Consider one or more of these biblical stories. How does relationship fuel the work to which God calls these persons? In each case, what barriers did they have to cross in order to be in relationship?

   Esau and Jacob. Genesis 32:9–12, 33:1–14

Joseph and his brothers. Genesis 37 and 42–45

Shiphrah and Puah. Exodus 1:8–21

Naomi and Ruth. Ruth 1

David and Jonathan. 1 Samuel 18:1–4, 19:1–7 and 20

Elijah and the widow. 1 Kings 17 (and Luke 4:24–26)

Jesus and Matthew the tax collector. Matthew 9:9

Philip and the eunuch. Acts 8:26–39

Closing

Review the "Practicing Foolishness" prompts below, which are aimed at helping us practice building relationships and discovering friends. If you're in a group, consider trying one of the role-playing scenarios in **2E** before you close your time together. Commit to one or more of the foolishness prompts you personally will do to practice what we explored in this session.

The Church Is More about Relationships Than Programs

If you're in a group, share prayer requests and be in prayer for one another during the coming week.

A prayer for ending each session:
> Holy and healing God, help us to trust you as we practice foolish love and ministry, this week and beyond. Send us out with courage and curiosity. Let us see those we meet with the eyes and grace of our Savior Jesus, in whose name we pray. Amen.

Practicing Foolishness

Here are some ideas for practicing the learnings of this section of *Foolish Church*. It will require some foolishness for us to *do* the things Lee describes. Let these prompts get you started and spark your own reckless imagination.

small folly

____**2A** Think about a friendship you have made in the past five years, outside of your family. If possible, call or get together with this person and talk about how you became friends. Consider the steps your relationship took from "acquaintance" to "friend" and how you became aware that had happened. What things did you do individually and together along the way? (If you cannot think of a friendship that has developed within those five years, think of some acquaintances you have made in that time and consider why a friendship has not developed.)

____**2B** Take a blank page and write down thirty things you could invite a friend to do with you. It may help you get to thirty if you think back over the things you've done with friends, or look at a community calendar and imagine things you might enjoy. Post your list in a prominent place like on your bathroom mirror or on your desktop where you'll see it often. Refer to it as you consider how to create new friendships in your life.

The Fools' Manual

____**2C** When you have a conversation with a random stranger, ask yourself, "What would it take to become friends with this person?" Notice how this question feels in you. Is it intriguing? And can you imagine it actually happening? If no, are *you* resisting that idea or do you imagine *they* would? Is it a question of time or mutual interests? If this feels more natural with some people and more uncomfortable with others, ask yourself why the difference. You don't have to befriend the person; just pay attention to how you respond to these questions, and why.

more reckless

____**2D** Invite a person you don't know well to do something from the list you created in **2B**. How does it feel to make the invitation? If they said yes, how was it? If they said no, consider how you feel about that, and then try inviting someone else.

____**2E** Invite a friend or small group to practice role-playing one or more of these scenarios. As you role-play, work on inviting the person without imposing judgment or feeling shame if they say *no*. Debrief with your friend or small group, and maybe practice a second time, perhaps changing roles this time, noticing how this feels and where it's hard.

- Invite the lonely person you noticed in your row on Sunday morning to join you for coffee or lunch.

- Notice the person who's sitting alone at church. Strike up a conversation with them afterward and invite them to the church picnic that's happening later this afternoon. Find out if they need a ride, and offer to make sure they have one.

- Reach out to the person who annoyed you recently over arriving late to the class you lead or missing the deadline for something they said they'd do. Don't focus on the conflict; just have a conversation, until you find out something you didn't already know about them, or some interest you have in common.

- Reach out to the person you know cares for an aging parent or a special needs child. Invite them to your coffee group that meets this week. If they say no, see if there's an accommodation that would help, like bringing the group to their place, or meeting at a different time. How can you express supportive care to this person?

The Church Is More about Relationships Than Programs

extreme foolishness

___**2F** Look for an opportunity to have a conversation with an adult who is being served by a local mission project. Resist the tendency to see them as a "needy person" who requires your help. Approach them instead as a whole human being, with a life, interests, and wisdom you know little about. How might your conversation draw that out, and help you both to see the humanity you share?

___**2G** Initiate a conversation with one or more leaders about a mission project and ask questions about how the project does (or could) build real relationships with the persons who are being served, rather than just helping at arm's length. Offer to lead a study on *Toxic Charity*, by Robert Lupton, or *When Helping Hurts*, by Corbett and Fikkert (as listed in the *Foolish Church* bibliography) as a way to explore these questions further.

___**2H** Create an opportunity to invite someone who makes you uncomfortable to a gathering at your home or other venue where you are the host. Don't put yourself at risk with someone who is not safe to be around, but do push the envelope a bit by including someone outside your natural circle of friends. This may work best if it's not just you and that person, but a friendly gathering of friends that you are expanding with this invitation. As you spend time together, how can you make room for that person?

___**2I** Talk with your pastor and/or other church leaders to explore how you might create opportunities for inviting new people into settings where you will get to know each other better. A monthly meet-up or shared meal where groups are matched differently each time can be a great opportunity to build relationship without an agenda. Can't get your leaders interested? You could start a tradition at a local restaurant by simply inviting people!

___**2J** _____
_____
_____
_____

The Fools' Manual

____2K_____

_____
_____
_____
_____

(This is your space to devise your own prompts, and then to practice them. How foolish will you get?)

> *So, what did you do? What worked, and what felt like it didn't? What did you learn? How foolish were you?! Take time to share your experiences and your J and K prompts by reporting on Facebook or Twitter using this hashtag: **#FoolishChurch**. Don't forget to check for others' ideas posted there as well. Lee will collect the best of these and share them on the Foolish Church page.*

Everything we do as a church hangs on love.

Lee Roorda Schott

Session 3

The Church Believes and Protects

> The easiest thing in the world is to *disbelieve her*. We do it when women say they've been raped and when girls say they've been abused. Our first question often is not, "How could he do that to you?" Instead, it's "What did you do to bring it on yourself?"
>
> *Lee Roorda Schott*

The Fools' Manual

Beginning

A question for entering this session:

> Describe a time when you were telling the truth and someone believed you, and it made a difference.

Share briefly about the foolishness prompts from session 2 that you (or others) tried. What happened? What did you learn?

This session focuses on chapter 3 of *Foolish Church*, which wants us to take seriously the responsibility of believing and standing up for one another, especially when those around us are injured or vulnerable.

A prayer as we open this time:

> O God, we are your beautiful people, and sometimes we can be extremely fragile. Help us bring that truth to this time today. Let us imagine loving one another foolishly enough that we would stand up for someone for whom we aren't responsible. Help us be a church that loves the way Jesus asks us to. Amen.

From the book

What stories or ideas in chapter 3 particularly spoke to you? Challenged you? Inspired you?

The Church Believes and Protects

Can you think of times when you or your church stood up for a person and then felt let down by them? Why did that happen? How did you work through it?

Read this excerpt from page 41 of *Foolish Church* and then consider the questions that follow:

> This is how truth emerges. We tell what we can. We tell what we are able to face, for now, or what we think you our listener is ready to bear, about what happened. Maybe we are absolutely clear that we shaded the facts a bit in our favor. Maybe we don't even realize we're doing it. But for that moment, at least, that's our story. We may tell it again later when we can face more of the truth, and our telling may shift. . . .
>
> And the role of the church in this scenario is to . . . be the one who hears the amount of truth that we can say today, and responds by believing us and encouraging us. Or at least *starts* with belief and encouragement, so that we know it was safe to share. The church must start with care and concern, rather than walls of doubt that try to talk us out of what we dared to put into words. There may be room later for truth-finding and re-examination. And very likely there *is* more to the story than we can tell right then. But especially in that first moment, to express care and support and a willingness to help? That's what The Church does for a hurting and broken world.

1. Have you ever doubted the story someone else shared with you? How did you respond? What considerations affected that response?

2. How might you stand with another person who claims to have been injured or mistreated as they pursue their next steps or remedies, even if you don't completely trust their story of what happened?

3. What should go into a church's decision (or our personal decisions) about who and what we'll stand up for?

4. How would your church be different if, as Lee says at page 41, "*We get to trust that the church is on our side*"?

From the Bible

Read and consider the Bible excerpt and reflection in the box at page 47 of *Foolish Church*.

Read these words from 1 Samuel 1 (and perhaps the entire chapter for context), and then consider the questions that follow:

> 9After they had eaten and drunk at Shiloh, Hannah rose and presented herself before the Lord. Now Eli the priest was sitting on the seat beside the doorpost of the temple of the Lord. 10She was deeply distressed and prayed to the Lord, and wept bitterly. . . .
>
> 12As she continued praying before the Lord, Eli observed her mouth. 13Hannah was praying silently; only her lips moved, but her voice was not heard; therefore Eli thought she was drunk. 14So Eli said to her, "How long will you make a drunken spectacle of yourself? Put away your wine." 15But Hannah answered, "No, my lord, I am a woman deeply troubled; I have drunk neither wine nor strong drink, but I have been pouring out my soul before the Lord. 16Do not regard your servant as a worthless woman, for I have been speaking out of my great anxiety and vexation all this time." 17Then Eli answered, "Go in peace; the God of Israel grant the petition you have made to him."

The Church Believes and Protects

1. Reading this account, does it surprise you that Eli responds to Hannah as he does? Can you think of other ways he might have approached this woman who was clearly in distress? What would have been a good opening question?

2. Can you remember a time you jumped to a conclusion about someone, without sufficient knowledge about their situation? How might you have handled that moment differently?

3. Hannah turns out to be a good advocate for her own needs in this moment. She tells the truth and Eli believes her. In your experience, is this typical? What factors might keep the person in Hannah's position from being able to be heard?

4. Consider one or more of these New Testament stories in which Jesus interacted with someone who might have appeared threatening or pushy. How does Jesus believe and protect the person? What questions does he ask?

    A leper. Mark 1:40–45

    The Samaritan woman at the well. John 4:5–42

    The Gerasene with an unclean spirit. Mark 5:1–20

The young man with a demon. Mark 9:14–29

The Syro-Phoenician woman. Matthew 15:21–18

Closing

Review the "Practicing Foolishness" prompts below. If you're in a group, consider trying one of the role-playing scenarios in **3E** before you close your time together. Commit to one or more of the foolishness prompts you personally will do to practice what we explored in this session.

If you're in a group, share prayer requests and be in prayer for one another during the coming week.

A prayer for ending each session:
> Holy and healing God, help us to trust you as we practice foolish love and ministry, this week and beyond. Send us out with courage and curiosity. Let us see those we meet with the eyes and grace of our Savior Jesus, in whose name we pray. Amen.

Practicing Foolishness

Here are some ideas for practicing the learnings of this section of *Foolish Church*. It will require some foolishness for us to *do* the things Lee describes. Let these prompts get you started and spark your own reckless imagination.

small folly

____**3A** As you go about your day, pay attention to the people and spaces around you, with curiosity and compassion. Do this without any expectation that you will *do* anything; just *notice*. Ask yourself what might be going on with that neighbor, or that co-worker. Listen for what they don't say. Watch their body language. (You'll find more on this idea at pages 44–45 of *Foolish Church*.) Become aware of how much you do or don't pay attention to these clues, and how likely you are to make favorable or unfavorable assumptions about people.

____**3B** Pick up today's newspaper, or scroll through your favorite social media feed, and see how many stories it contains of injustice, inequality, tragedy, and/or heartache. They won't all be labeled this way; you'll often have to look behind the printed story or post to notice the broken hearts or the wounded souls and, often, the institutionalized injustice, prejudice, or other brokenness underneath. Pay attention to your own reaction as you do this. What needs touch you more deeply? Tears or anger may be clues.

____**3C** When someone behaves badly, pause (before you react to them) to ask yourself this question: "What do you suppose happened to that person to make them act that way?" It's a useful question across a range of experiences, such as when someone cuts you off in traffic, when your colleague takes credit for your work, or when a family member loses their temper. Don't ask the question out loud, but pause to wonder. See if you can imagine an answer that, if true, would make you more compassionate toward the person. You don't have to know whether it's true; it's often enough to imagine a backstory that might make sense of the action you just witnessed. See if this exercise makes you feel more compassionate as you move through your day.

more reckless

____**3D** As you watch the news, or as you follow the prompts in **3B** above, imagine yourself standing next to the person going through one of these challenges. What do you wish you could say to them? Does it come from a place of love and caring? Can you find that space in yourself, where you could believe and protect that person as we've been exploring in this session? Does it help to imagine they're a member of your church?

____**3E** Invite a friend or small group to practice role-playing one or more of these scenarios. In each case, the person has come to your church on a Sunday morning and you've just become aware of their situation. What do you say to them? Debrief with your friend or small group, and maybe practice a second time, perhaps changing roles this time, noticing how this feels and where it's hard.

- The person with mental illness who was profiled in the newspaper this week in a story about people who can't afford their medication.
- The woman with bruises who says she's finally left him.
- The transgender friends that made the news after a landlord refused to rent to them.
- A person who owned the apartment building down the block that burned down this week, with two fatalities.
- A family member of a person who recently died in a drive-by shooting.
- A family member of a person recently arrested as the perpetrator in a drive-by shooting.

____**3F** Spend some time learning about an injustice or need you feel called to address. (You could start with one that evoked emotions as discussed in **3B**.) There are advocacy groups around any number of needs, ranging from poverty, to racism, to immigration, to criminal justice, to sexual assault, to animal cruelty, to the environment. Get online and learn about that subject, and find out who in your community is working to address it. Show up at a meeting or rally on this subject, and pay attention to the different ways people are tackling it. Notice how *you* feel moved to action. What skills or passions can you bring to this work?

____**3G** Call or write a lawmaker on a matter that concerns you. Reference a bill or issue, if possible, and communicate the specific action you want the lawmaker to take for or against it. If you can tell a story that illustrates the impact you are concerned about, that's even better.

extreme foolishness

____**3H** When you become aware of a person who needs help navigating a challenging issue, stand by them as they walk through it. Don't take

The Church Believes and Protects

over their responsibility and decisions, but encourage them and help them find their voice and access available resources. This might include helping someone advocate for their own health care, or helping her set up her apartment when she's leaving the halfway house, or maybe helping him navigate the public transportation system. You could find yourself at city hall with someone trying to complete a complex registration process. Having someone at our side can make the impossible seem manageable. Could you be that person?

____**3I** Talk to your pastor or church leaders about starting or strengthening an advocacy ministry through your local church. Many faith traditions have resources for persons who want to pursue this work. You could make good use of Bill Mefford's book, *The Fig Tree Revolution* (see the *Foolish Church* bibliography). Community-based organizers are often linked to local churches. Help people make the connection between faith and the justice issues affecting your community.

____**3J** _____
_____
_____
_____
_____

____**3K** _____
_____
_____
_____

(This is your space to devise your own prompts, and then to practice them. How foolish will you get?)

*So, what did you do? What worked, and what felt like it didn't? What did you learn? How foolish were you?! Take time to share your experiences and your J and K prompts by reporting on Facebook or Twitter using this hashtag: **#FoolishChurch**. Don't forget to check for others' ideas posted there as well. Lee will collect the best of these and share them on the Foolish Church page.*

The Fools' Manual

The church must be prepared to stand with persons who are being battered by the world.

Lee Roorda Schott

Session 4

The Church Builds Boundaries, Not Walls

> A church that does not have good boundaries will never be able to let down its walls and offer a free and gracious welcome. Good boundaries are an integral element of a church set free to love well.
>
> *Lee Roorda Schott*

The Fools' Manual

Beginning

A question for entering this session:

> Recall a time someone clarified what the boundaries were in a relationship or a social or business setting. How did that feel?

Share briefly about the foolishness prompts from session 3 that you (or others) tried. What happened? What did you learn?

This session focuses on chapter 4 of *Foolish Church*, which names the paradoxical imperative of the church tearing down walls that would keep people out, while establishing good boundaries that will keep our togetherness healthy.

A prayer as we open this time:

> O God, we are your beautiful people who seek to be healthy in community with one another. Help us bring that truth to this time today. Let us imagine loving one another so foolishly that no one is excluded, and each can claim what they need to be well. Help us be a church that loves the way Jesus asks us to. Amen.

From the book

What stories or ideas in chapter 4 particularly spoke to you? Challenged you? Inspired you?

Take a hard look at your church—its space, its people, its life together—and make two lists: (1) who is welcomed and (2) who doesn't belong. These

The Church Builds Boundaries, Not Walls

categories may not be overtly expressed, but what can you discern about your church's answers?

Read this excerpt from page 57 of *Foolish Church* and then consider the questions that follow:

> A church's resolve to eliminate walls and remain open and hospitable to all comers will paradoxically depend on good boundaries. We cannot maintain an increasingly diverse and welcoming space without some clarity on what belongs to each side of these new relationships.
>
> Good boundaries will keep us from taking on too much of [another person's] problems. They'll help us say what we're willing to do to help, and they'll help us clarify, unashamed, that there are things we won't do.
>
> We may encounter behaviors that cross a line, and we will need to address them. . . . When a person's behavior becomes disruptive to the worship or work we seek to do together, good boundaries will clarify what is permissible and what is not. Our community's life together depends on responding appropriately so that all may thrive.

1. If you ran the world—or just your church—whom would you find it hard to welcome? (Yes, it's OK to admit that some people are challenging.) Pause and ask yourself: why those people? What is it about them? What are you worried about?

2. Looking at the list you just wrote, how might it make you more willing to welcome those people if you were sure your church (its pastor(s), leaders, staff, and influential members) had clear boundaries that would be fairly and consistently implemented, as described in chapter 4 of *Foolish Church*?

3. Have you ever gotten caught on one side of a boundary problem, where someone was too wrapped up in your business or you were taking too much responsibility for theirs? Recall those circumstances and how it felt to be so intertwined.

4. What past experiences with boundaries make it hard for you or your church to imagine healthy boundaries going forward?

5. How would your church be different if, as Lee says at page 60, "*The Church is always open with no limits, and it expresses its welcome in part through healthy boundaries*"?

From the Bible
Read and consider the Bible excerpt and reflection in the box at page 63 of *Foolish Church*.

Read these words from Luke 19 and then consider the questions that follow:

> 1[Jesus] entered Jericho and was passing through it. 2A man was there named Zacchaeus; he was a chief tax collector and was rich. 3He was trying to see who Jesus was, but on account of the crowd he could not, because he was short in stature. 4So he ran ahead and climbed a sycamore tree to see him, because he was going to pass that way. 5When Jesus came to the place, he looked up and said to him, "Zacchaeus, hurry and come down; for I must stay at your house today." 6So he hurried down and was happy to welcome him. 7All who saw it began to grumble and said, "He has gone to be the guest of one who is a sinner."8Zacchaeus stood there and said to the Lord, "Look, half of my possessions, Lord, I

The Church Builds Boundaries, Not Walls

will give to the poor; and if I have defrauded anyone of anything, I will pay back four times as much." 9Then Jesus said to him, "Today salvation has come to this house, because he too is a son of Abraham. 10For the Son of Man came to seek out and to save the lost."

1. What walls have the townspeople erected against Zacchaeus? Can you tell why? How are those walls communicated?

2. Does Jesus stay within those walls? Why or why not?

3. What behavior (if any) does Jesus require from Zacchaeus in return for Jesus' willingness to associate with him? Does Zacchaeus promise to change because he's required to? Out of gratitude? For some other reason?

4. Consider one or more of these Bible stories. In what ways did Jesus break down walls and expectations in order to pursue his ministry?

   The man with the withered hand. Mark 3:1–6

   The woman with a hemorrhage. Mark 5:24–34

   Eating with a Pharisee. Luke 7:36 and 14:1

Eating with tax collectors and sinners. Matthew 9:10–13 and Luke 15

The woman with an alabaster jar. Mark 7:36–50

Welcoming children. Matthew 19:13–15

Woman, behold your son. John 19:25b–27

5. Consider one or more of these Bible stories. Notice the way Jesus set up boundaries in order to stay well in his own ministry.

Going aside to a quiet place to pray. Mark 1:35, Luke 5:15–16

Taking disciples with him for rest. Mark 6:30–34

"Get behind me, Satan!" Matthew 16:21–23

"Not mine to grant" who will sit where in the kingdom. Mark 10:35–40

"Neither will I tell you." Luke 20:1–8

Garden of Gethsemane. Matthew 26:36–44

The Church Builds Boundaries, Not Walls

Closing

Review the "Practicing Foolishness" prompts below. If you're in a group, consider trying one of the role-playing scenarios in **4E** before you close your time together. Commit to one or more of the foolishness prompts you personally will do to practice what we explored in this session.

If you're in a group, share prayer requests and be in prayer for one another during the coming week.

A prayer for ending each session:
> Holy and healing God, help us to trust you as we practice foolish love and ministry, this week and beyond. Send us out with courage and curiosity. Let us see those we meet with the eyes and grace of our Savior Jesus, in whose name we pray. Amen.

Practicing Foolishness

Here are some ideas for practicing the learnings of this section of *Foolish Church*. It will require some foolishness for us to *do* the things Lee describes. Let these prompts get you started and spark your own reckless imagination.

small folly

____**4A** Today as you come across other human beings, practice saying "yes" to them. Say it under your breath, or in your head. Say it even if they make you uncomfortable. You don't have to say "yes" if they ask you to do something, but say it to yourself, about that person, as a discipline of welcome and acceptance. Say it as a reminder that God says *yes* to every one of us. What if we started every encounter with *yes*?

____**4B** Practice noticing where your boundaries end and the next person's begin. This happens in various ways. One person may stand too close. Another will try to make something your problem when it isn't. Or they'll speak for you, or over you. Maybe they'll expect you to do something you don't want to do. Pay attention, too, to the ways you might do these things to those around you. How does it feel when someone steps on your boundary, or when you realize you've crossed theirs? How does it feel when boundaries are respected?

____**4C** Think about your church and make a list of the things expected of persons who wish to be part of the faith community. How should they dress? How must they act? What rules are commonly recognized even if they are not said out loud? Walk around and through your space and look at your printed and online materials to identify any expectations you might have missed. Review this list and consider whether these expectations line up with the gospel.

more reckless

____**4D** Invite another person from your church to do what you did under 4C. When they're ready, compare notes. What did one of you see that the other didn't? Can you agree on a list that represents the church's expectations? Do you think it's in line with what Jesus would do? Consider expanding this process to include more people, and more diverse people. Notice how that changes the conversation.

____**4E** Invite a friend or small group to practice role-playing one or more of these scenarios in which you wish to say "no" to the request being made. Practice saying no. Experiment with how much information to give about why you're saying "no." Can you do it? How does the conversation change when you say a simple "no," versus when you explain your answer? Debrief with your friend or small group, and maybe practice a second time, perhaps changing roles this time, noticing how this feels and where it's hard.

- Your friend asks you to go to the mall with them. You enjoy going to the mall, but can't today because of a deadline for a college assignment.
- Same as above, but this friend has done a lot of favors for you in the past.
- Same as above, but you and this friend have sometimes been bad influences on each other, including using drugs together.

The Church Builds Boundaries, Not Walls

- An elderly, indiscreet member of your church asks you to help with some yard work. You've done this before. But you cannot this time, because of some health concerns you are not ready to share.
- Your son calls with a last-minute request for you to watch the toddlers. You have other plans with friends who have come in from out of town. Your son sounds desperate.
- Same as above, but your son was recently diagnosed with mental illness and you have been worried about him and the kids.
- Someone invites you to a party where you think there will be drugs and alcohol, and you're trying hard to stay clean and sober.
- A co-worker that you admire invites you to come with them to an event across state lines. If you go, it will violate the terms of your parole. Your colleague doesn't know your criminal history.

extreme foolishness

____**4F** Initiate a conversation with your pastor or your church's leaders with the aim of identifying what your rightful expectations are, as suggested at page 61 of *Foolish Church*. You might use this list as a starting point for that conversation. Will your church welcome the following people? (If you will not welcome them, go back and reread chapter 4!) If you will welcome them but some boundaries need to be established, what are they? Who should be responsible to know these answers, and to have those conversations?

- She's wearing a swastika on her T-shirt.
- He has no shoes or shirt.
- She is covered with tattoos.
- His clothing and behavior make you certain he is gay.
- You're confused about what their gender is.
- She's clearly under the influence of drugs or alcohol.
- They smell bad, like an incontinent person.
- They smell bad, and appear to be homeless.
- They're a _____ (*Republican* or *Democrat*) (whichever is most out of step with your community).
- She talks very softly and you have trouble understanding her.

- He appears to have dementia and acts disoriented.
- She is not fluent in any language used in your church.
- He is deaf.
- She talks loudly and interrupts worship.
- He's someone you know was recently released from prison.
- She's on a sex offender registry.
- He is visibly carrying a gun, or tells you he has one.
- He's carrying a backpack that looks like it might have a gun in it.

____**4G** Practice speaking the truth in love, in a matter-of-fact way, in a situation where someone just crossed a boundary with you, or with the church. Be fair and don't single out one person if multiple people are involved. Focus on something that just happened, rather than dredging up ancient history. State directly and calmly what you're concerned about, and if a boundary needs to be named, name it. Pay attention to how this feels, in your body and in the room.

____**4H** Talk to your pastor or church leaders about how to more fully communicate and live out your no-walls welcome to persons in your community. Is there room to soften some of the expectations you identified in **4C**, **4D**, and **4F**? Who in your church needs to be part of this larger discussion? Work on clarifying and expanding the "yes" you are able to offer as a church.

____**4I** In that awkward moment when someone who deserves to be welcomed is experiencing informal walls of criticism, exclusion, or other "no" messages from people in your church, do something visible to help that person know there is room for them. Sit down next to them, or pull up a chair at that table that looks full already. Treat them the way you'd treat a friend, and do so visibly and purposefully. Make introductions if that's appropriate, and exert some effort to include them in the conversation that was excluding them. Smile, and be the pleasant guide you would want in a similar situation.

The Church Builds Boundaries, Not Walls

___4J _____
_____
_____
_____

___4K _____
_____
_____
_____

(This is your space to devise your own prompts, and then to practice them. How foolish will you get?)

*So, what did you do? What worked, and what felt like it didn't? What did you learn? How foolish were you?! Take time to share your experiences and your J and K prompts by reporting on Facebook or Twitter using this hashtag: **#FoolishChurch**. Don't forget to check for others' ideas posted there as well. Lee will collect the best of these and share them on the Foolish Church page.*

I believe, and I say with great earnestness to my sisters in prison, "There is a church that is *longing* to be gracious to you." I desperately hope I'm right.

Lee Roorda Schott

SESSION 5

The Church Brings Its Messes into the Light

> We settle for repeatedly diminished expectations in which relationships within the church are less honest and more fractured than they were meant to be. We haven't even noticed that we fall short of a higher ideal, because we have lost track of that possibility.
>
> *Lee Roorda Schott*

The Church Brings Its Messes into the Light

Beginning

A question for entering this session:

> Recall a time a time you had a conflict with another person and it was resolved, and your relationship was restored.

Share briefly about the foolishness prompts from session 4 that you (or others) tried. What happened? What did you learn?

This session focuses on chapter 5 of *Foolish Church*, which highlights the biblical intention and the process Jesus gives us to live in peace with each other within the church. What if we took this process seriously? What would it look like where we are?

A prayer as we open this time:

> O God, we are your beautiful people whose relationships get distorted again and again, and we forget how to be at peace with one another. Help us bring that truth to this time today. Let us imagine loving one another so foolishly that we would expect to resolve the issues that arise in our midst, and to help that happen. We want to become a people known for the resiliency of our life together. Help us be a church that loves the way Jesus asks us to. Amen.

From the book

What stories or ideas in chapter 5 particularly spoke to you? Challenged you? Inspired you?

The Fools' Manual

Can you describe a time when a conflict arose within the church and was resolved with intentionality and grace, where relationships were restored and love was manifest throughout the process? Describe what happened, and what made it possible in that instance. If you don't have an answer, why do you think that's the case?

Read this excerpt from page 79 of *Foolish Church* and then consider the questions that follow:

> False community is what you have when people are nice on the surface and don't address the truth of what is going on underneath. It's the church where rumors and anger abound but are never addressed. True community is what you reach once you tackle the rumors and get to the bottom of them, and figure out whether anger is justified and what to do about it. True community emerges when a person can stop hiding the truth about herself and discover that she can still be valued, can still contribute her gifts, and can have an ongoing role in a community that wants her to be there.

1. Can you think of settings (in church or otherwise) in which you have experienced false and true community in this way? Identify those settings and consider how it feels to live within them. Where did you feel safe, valued, and whole?

2. Getting from false community to true community requires us to pay a price, in facing conflict and speaking the truth to one another. What are your experiences with this? When have you been willing to pay that cost?

The Church Brings Its Messes into the Light

3. Describe your church's expectation for resolving conflict, and its plan for helping that happen. Do you personally have such an expectation and plan, in your own relationships? Do these plans get followed?

4. How would your church be different if, as Lee says at page 77, "*The church responds to misbehavior and division with intentional movement toward accountability, resolution, and renewed relationship*"?

From the Bible

Read and consider the Bible excerpt and reflection in the box at page 80 of *Foolish Church*.

Read these words from 2 Samuel 12:5–7, 13, which are part of a larger story of King David's sinful taking of Bathsheba, which you'll find in 2 Samuel 11:1–12:15, and then consider the questions that follow:

> 5Then David's anger was greatly kindled against the man. He said to Nathan, "As the Lord lives, the man who has done this deserves to die; 6he shall restore the lamb fourfold, because he did this thing, and because he had no pity." 7Nathan said to David, "You are the man! . . ." 13David said to Nathan, "I have sinned against the Lord."

The Fools' Manual

1. Does it surprise you that King David, one of the greatest heroes of the Bible, is found to have become embroiled in sin? Take a moment to recall David's sin in this episode with Bathsheba, including his efforts to cover it up.

2. Can you recall a time in your own life when you (like David) couldn't see your own sin? How did you react when someone pointed it out?

3. What would be needed for the church to be trusted to help us identify our sin, resolve conflict among ourselves, and restore us to loving relationships with one another and with God?

4. Consider one or more of these biblical stories in which persons were called to account and/or invited to return to loving relationship with one another. What do these stories tell us about what God wants for today's church?

    Jonah. Jonah 1:1–3:3

    Zechariah. Luke 1:8–23

    Martha (sister of Mary). Luke 10:38–42

    Doubting Thomas. John 20:24–29

The Church Brings Its Messes into the Light

Ananias and Sapphira. Acts 5:1–11

Read again these words from Matthew 18 that give us a blueprint for seeking reconciliation, and consider the questions that follow:

> 15"If another member of the church sins against you, go and point out the fault when the two of you are alone. If the member listens to you, you have regained that one. 16But if you are not listened to, take one or two others along with you, so that every word may be confirmed by the evidence of two or three witnesses. 17If the member refuses to listen to them, tell it to the church; and if the offender refuses to listen even to the church, let such a one be to you as a Gentile and a tax collector.

1. Have you been part of a community that regularly seeks to live by these words? If so, describe that experience. If not, why do you think we disregard this instruction from Jesus?

2. Lee describes how this instruction from Matthew 18 guides the way the church council inside the prison seeks to resolve conflict (*Foolish Church* at 67–73, and appendix 4). Is it realistic to think a similar process could work in churches outside of prison? Why or why not?

Closing

Review the "Practicing Foolishness" prompts below. If you're in a group, consider trying one of the role-playing scenarios in **5E** before you close your time together. Commit to one or more of the foolishness prompts you personally will do to practice what we explored in this session.

If you're in a group, share prayer requests and be in prayer for one another during the coming week.

A prayer for ending each session:

> Holy and healing God, help us to trust you as we practice foolish love and ministry, this week and beyond. Send us out with courage and curiosity. Let us see those we meet with the eyes and grace of our Savior Jesus, in whose name we pray. Amen.

Practicing Foolishness

Here are some ideas for practicing the learnings of this section of *Foolish Church*. It will require some foolishness for us to *do* the things Lee describes. Let these prompts get you started and spark your own reckless imagination.

small folly

____**5A** Pay attention to the small and large conflicts that affect or concern you. This could include old and new conflicts in your most intimate relationships, fleeting annoyances that arise as you bump into strangers, ongoing conflict in the workplace, church, or community, and even political and cultural conflicts that play out on a global stage. Make note of (1) the feelings these conflicts evoke, and where you feel them in your body; (2) whether and how you seek to address and resolve the conflict on the spot or, if you don't, why you don't; (3) your strategies for addressing the conflict itself or your anxiety about it, especially if it's one you cannot personally resolve; and (4) which conflicts are worth addressing and why. What do you notice about your reaction to and interaction with conflict?

____**5B** Sit down with a blank page and make a list of the conflicts that have arisen in your life. What relationships have you abandoned? Which friends do you no longer contact? Whom have you blocked on social media? With curiosity but not judgment, consider the relationships on this list

The Church Brings Its Messes into the Light

and what led to that brokenness. Did you try to seek reconciliation? If so, what worked, or didn't? If you didn't try, why not? Survey the list and ask yourself whether it's worth seeking reconciliation of any of these relationships. If you dare, pray and ask Jesus to answer that question for you.

____ **5C** Sit with someone from your church and together make a list of conflicts that have affected your life together as a church, recently or long ago. Note whether and how they were resolved, if they were. Did the church follow a process? Did someone leave the church? Identify the impact this conflict has had on the church's ministry, on individuals, and on relationships within the church. Wonder aloud if these conflicts burden your church's ministry even today.

more reckless

____ **5D** Seek out a conversation with a person involved in a long-ago conflict in your life (not necessarily with you) or in your church. Explore what happened and how it has affected that person and/or your church in the time since it happened. Did they seek resolution? Ask questions about the process. What do they wish had happened?

____ **5E** Invite a friend or small group to practice role-playing one or more of the following scenarios in which you have an opportunity to practice a Matthew 18 process for addressing a conflict. Pay special attention to whether any consequences need to be imposed as a result of the situation. Debrief with your friend or small group, and maybe practice a second time, perhaps changing roles this time, noticing how this feels and where it's hard.

- Two longstanding members are arguing over who gets to make decisions about how to arrange the church kitchen.
- Your church's biggest giver says she will stop giving if the building plan goes forward.
- A boy in your youth group brings a friend who says he's an atheist. The youth leader asks that atheist friend not to come back. These friends and a couple of others say they're quitting the youth group over this.
- A member of your leadership group fails to maintain confidentiality about your custodian's recent diagnosis with cancer.
- One of your lead musicians and her husband are getting a divorce. Rumor says she was having an affair. Some church members are calling

The Fools' Manual

for her to step down from leadership. Both are actively involved in the church, along with their children. People are beginning to take sides.

____**5F** Initiate conversation with your pastor or church leaders about instituting a Matthew 18 process for conflict resolution within your church. Advocate for the church to adopt both the intention and a plan for remaining at peace with one another. (See appendix 4 of *Foolish Church* for an example from Lee's ministry.)

extreme recklessness

____**5G** Follow what Jesus said in Matthew 18 to address a conflict that *you* are part of. Have the conversation with the other person. If that doesn't resolve it, bring one or two others into the conversation. And so forth. Go into this process prayerfully and with the expectation that the issue can be resolved. Pay attention to what you learn along the way.

____**5H** If someone has wronged you but you *aren't* willing to go through the Matthew 18 process, then let it go. Stop talking with others about it. Seek to forgive them for your sake, if not for theirs. Some relationships will need to be released rather than renewed, for your safety and peace of mind. Where they can be renewed, do your part to seek reconciliation.

____**5I** Use your voice to redirect a conversation that feels inconsistent with Matthew 18. Stay out of conversations *about* people and, instead, encourage the complainer to take up the issue directly with the person involved. Don't become an intermediary between two people who are upset with each other but, if appropriate, offer to sit with them while they talk about the issue. Don't be self-righteous or sanctimonious about it, but do what you can to change the atmosphere within your church.

____**5J** _____
_____
_____
_____

____**5K** _____
_____

The Church Brings Its Messes into the Light

(This is your space to devise your own prompts, and then to practice them. How foolish will you get?)

So, what did you do? What worked, and what felt like it didn't? What did you learn? How foolish were you?! Take time to share your experiences and your J and K prompts by reporting on Facebook or Twitter using this hashtag: **#FoolishChurch**. *Don't forget to check for others' ideas posted there as well. Lee will collect the best of these and share them on the Foolish Church page.*

At the heart of all this is *forgiveness*. Are we willing to hold one another accountable and offer forgiveness when that is due, or aren't we? . . . Forgiveness has the capacity to change the world.

Lee Roorda Schott

Session 6

The Church Has Something Critically Important to Offer

> I no longer think silence is an adequate response when someone says she's given up on church, or that she can't believe in God anymore. I want to be ready to ask why, to really listen to her story, and perhaps to explain why I *still* go to church, and how the God I know still commands my devotion. If we who are faithful Christians aren't ready to claim these truths, in words, face to face with people we know, who will?
>
> Lee Roorda Schott

The Church Has Something Critically Important to Offer

Beginning

A question for entering this session:

> Tell one happy memory you have of church.

Share briefly about the foolishness prompts from session 5 that you (or others) tried. What happened? What did you learn?

This session focuses on chapter 6 of *Foolish Church,* and the Conclusion. Chapter 6 invites us to focus on *why* church: Why does it matter? Who's it for? How clear are we about that? The Conclusion reminds us the church is called to be a "community and love and forgiveness." What a powerful, challenging assignment!

A prayer as we open this time:

> O God, we are your beautiful people whom you have gathered into your body, the church, and we don't always remember why. Help us bring that truth to this time today. Let us imagine loving one another so foolishly that we would lavishly welcome others into our fellowship, knowing that we all will be enriched by each other's presence. Help us be a church that loves the way Jesus asks us to. Amen.

From the book

What stories or ideas in chapter 6 and the Conclusion particularly spoke to you? Challenged you? Inspired you?

The Fools' Manual

What is important to you about being part of a church? What keeps you going or, if you have stopped, what were you missing?

Read this excerpt from page 79 of *Foolish Church* and then consider the questions that follow:

> God must long for us as churches to make room for people whose experiences and scars equip them to meet the needs of the overlooked and hidden communities that surround our churches. . . . God must wonder when we will make room for them and then let their experiences become a source of wisdom and solace not just for each other, but for us who have been there all along. We all will be stronger when we learn to make room, and let the intricacies of our many scars be joined into the beauty of life together. We will learn from one another how to speak the timeless truth of God's love and grace *into* and not just *around* the hardest moments of people's lives.

1. How have people made room for *you* to be part of the church you're currently attending, or one or more from your past? Was there something about you that was challenging? Reflect on how it felt to come new into a church.

2. How has your experience of church been enriched by the presence of people you likely wouldn't have met elsewhere?

3. What would it take for you to give up some of what you enjoy about your church in order to make room for people who think it's not *for* them?

The Church Has Something Critically Important to Offer

4. How would your church be different if, as Lee says at page 96, *"Our churches make space for incarnational ministry with, by, and through people longing for what The Church in its fullness has to offer"*?

From the Bible

Read and consider the Bible excerpt and reflection in the box at page 99 of *Foolish Church*.

Read these words of Jesus from Matthew 18, which Jesus speaks to his disciples, and consider the questions that follow:

> 18Truly I tell you, whatever you bind on earth will be bound in heaven, and whatever you loose on earth will be loosed in heaven. 19Again, truly I tell you, if two of you agree on earth about anything you ask, it will be done for you by my Father in heaven.

1. How does the church "bind" or "loose" by its actions? Can you think of examples where you have seen that happen through your church's ministry?

2. What do you hope for, through your ministries: *binding* or *loosing*? Having ministered inside a prison for so long, and noticing so many church walls that have kept people out, Lee definitely leans on the side of *loosing*! How about you, and why?

3. When you walk into the church, or pursue ministry there, or have a conversation with someone, or hurry past them to get where you're going, do you think of your actions as having consequences both here on earth and also in heaven? How does that affect what you do?

4. Consider one or more of these passages that might be read to speak of freeing or binding. How can the church enter into this work with intention and faithfulness?

   Lord of the Sabbath. Mark 2:23–28

   Jesus' commission. Luke 4:16–20

   "My yoke is easy and my burden is light." Matthew 11:28–30

   Tying, gathering, and scattering. Matthew 12:29–30, 13:30, 22:13

   "The truth will make you free." John 8:31–36

   Freeing a woman bound by Satan. Luke 13:10–17

   Raising and unbinding Lazarus. John 11:38–44

   "For freedom Christ has set us free." Galatians 5:1

Closing

Review the "Practicing Foolishness" prompts below. If you're in a group, consider trying one of the role-playing scenarios in **6E** before you close your time together. Commit to one or more of the foolishness prompts you personally will do to practice what we explored in this session.

If you're in a group, share prayer requests and be in prayer for one another as you continue to practice the foolishness to which God calls us, together.

A prayer as we complete the final session of this *Fools' Manual*:

> Holy and healing God, help us to trust you as we practice foolish love and ministry, buoyed by the learnings of this time and guided by your Spirit. Send us into this ongoing work with courage and curiosity. Help us love so freely and so well that we see it overflow through our churches and even through our own selves. Give us the holy gift of joy as we rearrange our churches and our lives to make room for your people, and watch us marvel as we become precious to one another. We pray all this in the power and grace of our Savior Jesus, in whose name we pray. Amen.

Practicing Foolishness

Here are some ideas for practicing the learnings of this section of *Foolish Church*. It will require some foolishness for us to *do* the things Lee describes. Let these prompts get you started and spark your own reckless imagination.

small folly

____**6A** Ask five people why they do or do not go to church. If it seems possible, ask them a second time, and maybe a third, and invite them to go deeper, because people's initial response may be glib. If they seem willing,

The Fools' Manual

ask them what kind of church they'd *love* to be part of. How do their answers help clarify your own thoughts on the critical importance of what the church offers?

____**6B** Consider and perhaps journal about this question, or discuss it with a church friend: Why would someone want to come to *your* church? Imagine inviting someone, and then answering their question *why*. Is what happens in your church *worth* inviting someone to, who isn't already part of it? If not, what would it take?

____**6C** Do you know your neighbors? And does your church know the people who live closest to it? Do a quick review of the ten households closest to you and your church. Don't just concentrate on the ones whose homes look just like yours; see what and who is actually there. Do you know the names of all the persons who live there? Do you know anything of their life stories, where they came from, what they do? What can you tell about their hopes, dreams, motivations, and fears?[1] Write down what you already know and, while you're at it, jot down ten ideas for how you might get to know these people better.

more reckless

____**6D** *Do* one or more of the ten ideas you wrote down in answer to 6C. See if that doesn't change how much you know of your neighbors, and how interested you are in their well-being. If it feels possible, take the initiative to invite them to your church, and be prepared to explain why you think they might want to be there.

____**6E** Invite a friend or small group to practice role-playing one or more of the conversations below, which could well happen if you are doing the foolishness we have discussed through these sessions! How can you acknowledge and honor a person's discomfort with change, impose healthy boundaries where needed, and not let negative reactions derail the gospel work you've undertaken? Debrief with your friend or small group, and maybe practice a second time, perhaps changing roles this time, noticing how this feels and where it's hard.

---

1. I am indebted to Jay Pathak and Dave Runyon for this idea, at pages 36 through 39 of *The Art of Neighboring: Building Genuine Relationships Right Outside Your Door* (as listed in the *Foolish Church* bibliography).

The Church Has Something Critically Important to Offer

- "You have to do something about the woman making all that noise in the front row."
- "Where did all these _____tattoos_____ come from?" (or fill in the blank with a different word, like wheelchairs, or poor people, or, well, you can supply your own).
- "I'm sorry if it makes me a bad person. But I won't stay here if you let that sex offender come."
- "I know we have this new conflict policy, and I'm supposed to talk about how Jim offended me. But it's nobody's business if I'm mad at Jim."
- "I just want my old church back."

____**6F** We haven't talked very specifically about a few categories of welcome that are critically important, such as young people, persons who identify as LGBTQIA, and persons whose race or ethnicity differs from most of your community. Reflect with your pastor and church leaders about this question: How will the things we've discussed in these sessions affect our welcome of those individuals? Is there additional organizational, theological, and/or cultural work we need to do in order to prepare ourselves to be the church they'll want to be part of? Get that work added to your church's priorities.

extreme recklessness

____**6G** Root out language in your church that makes a division between "us" and "them." Pay attention to the assumptions our words betray about who's in the room, and who isn't. Ask: Would you say it that way if you thought that person was sitting next to you? Use words like "neighbors," "friends," and "brothers and sisters"; it changes the way we think.

____**6H** Research who in your community might have trouble getting to church (like Jamie in the story Lee tells in chapter 6). Develop a ministry to help those folks join you in worship and other programs. Don't balk—like Lee did—when it grows.

____**6I** Make room for voices that aren't currently being heard in your church, whether that's in your worship services, your leadership groups, Christian education, or other conversations that happen there. How could

The Fools' Manual

we make time, on a regular basis, for persons to be heard who are undergoing or have survived life circumstances many of us have never faced? Our churches typically privilege a few voices, based on education, credentials, and insistence. Some of us will have to quiet ourselves if we're going to leave space for a broader definition of wisdom to be spoken, preferably by persons who are already becoming part of us. Let's become curators who seek out this beauty and help others discover it as well.

____6J _____
_____
_____
_____
_____

____6K _____
_____
_____
_____
_____

(This is your space to devise your own prompts, and then to practice them. How foolish will you get?)

So, what did you do? What worked, and what felt like it didn't? What did you learn? How foolish were you?! Take time to share your experiences and your J and K prompts by reporting on Facebook or Twitter using this hashtag: **#FoolishChurch***. Don't forget to check for others' ideas posted there as well. Lee will collect the best of these and share them on the Foolish Church page.*

What couldn't God do through a church foolish enough to be thrown open . . . ? I'm pretty certain Jesus would be in *that* place, with *those* people, having *those* conversations.

Lee Roorda Schott

About the Author

Lee is the foolish, grateful pastor of Women at the Well, a church inside the walls of the Iowa women's prison in Mitchellville, Iowa. For eight years she has worked with the women there as they pursue together the vision of *leading the church in love that breaks down walls*. This work has transformed her into an author, a frequent speaker outside the prison, an advocate, and a fool in all the good (and often challenging) ways she uses that term in her work.

Lee previously served as co-pastor of Polk City United Methodist Church in a small town just outside the Des Moines metro area. A 2007 graduate, with honors, of Saint Paul School of Theology in Kansas City, Missouri, Lee was ordained an elder in the United Methodist Church in 2009.

Lee's ministry career follows what she thought would be a career in law. After college at the University of Iowa, she went east to Harvard Law School and then began her career at Hahn Loeser & Parks, a private law firm in Cleveland, Ohio. In 1995 she and her family moved home to Iowa, where she worked as an in-house lawyer and eventually General Counsel at AmerUs Life Insurance Company. A lifelong United Methodist, she sensed a call from God after she began praying in earnest at the age of nearly forty.

A mom with three (grown) sons, Lee resides with her husband on her family's century farm near Prairie City. Contact her at foolishchurch@gmail.com or through the Foolish Church page on Facebook.

www.ingramcontent.com/pod-product-compliance
Lightning Source LLC
LaVergne TN
LVHW041309080426
835510LV00009B/916